First published in 2026 by

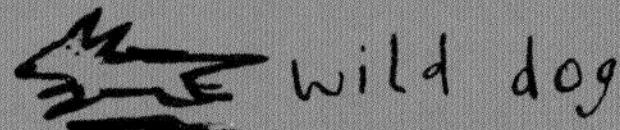

Melbourne, Australia
wdog.com.au

ISBN: 978-1-74203-726-4

10 9 8 7 6 5 4 3 2 1   26 27 28 29 30

Printed and bound in China by Everbest Printing Investment Limited.

Wild Dog would like to thank Dr Charlie Huveneers, research leader of Flinders University's Southern Shark Ecology Group, and Dr Adrian Gutteridge from the Marine Stewardship Council for their careful fact checking.

A catalogue record for this book is available from the National Library of Australia

FSC® is a non-profit international organisation established to promote the responsible management of the world's forests.

Image Credits: front cover wildestanimal; p2 Serhii Shcherbyna; pp4–5 Andrea Izzotti; pp6–7 Sergey Uryadnikov; pp8–9 Tomas Kotouc; p9 (inset, top left) Will Falcon; p9 (inset, bottom left) Animalgraphy; p9 (inset, right) Core.ou; p10 (inset) Yann hubert; p11 Osman Temizel, pp12–13 Chloe Langton, pp12–13 (background) Liami; p12 (inset, right) BMCL; pp14–15 Jennifer Mellon Photos; p15 (inset) Tomas Kotouc; pp16–17 C E Newman; p17 (inset) Kewin Lorenzen; pp18–19 Brandenburg; p18 (inset) Sardaka / Wikimedia Commons / CC-BY-3.0; pp20–21 VisionDive; pp22–23 FOODIES ACADEMY; pp24–25 ilikeyellow; pp26–27 Martin Voeller; pp28–29 Martin Voeller; p31 Serhii Shcherbyna; back cover Yann hubert

SHARKS

UP CLOSE

AIDAN GREEN

GREAT WHITE SHARK

Sharks have been around for a long time — more than 400 million years. They have outlived dinosaurs and survived several mass extinctions. Sharks are essential to the health of marine **ECOSYSTEMS**, but many species are now at risk due to overfishing.

There are more than 500 **SPECIES** of shark alive today. They range in size from the 20-centimetre dwarf lantern shark to the whale shark, which can grow up to 18 metres. Sharks live in most ocean habitats, from tropic reefs to the deep sea, and even under Arctic sea ice.

GREAT WHITE SHARK
GOBLIN SHARK
WHALE SHARK

Some species of shark are solitary hunters. Others **AGGREGATE** to feed, mate or shelter, or even gather in social groups of the same size, age and sex. Lemon sharks are more likely to swim with other sharks they know well, as opposed to strangers.

Certain fish live alongside sharks for food or shelter. Pilot fish gather around sharks and eat leftover food. Barber fish eat parasites from the hammerhead shark's skin. Remora fish attach themselves to sharks' bodies. Mackerel bump against a shark's rough skin to scratch off loose scales and parasites.

LEMON SHARKS

OCEANIC WHITETIP SHARK

Some sharks lay eggs but most give birth to live young. The number of live young can range from 2 pups for the bigeye thresher and up to 300 for the whale shark.

While most fish release sperm and millions of eggs into the water, sharks practise internal **FERTILISATION**. For some species, eggs hatch inside the mother shark.

SHARK EGG CASE

Shark eggs come in a variety of shapes, colours and textures. Long tendrils on an egg case tangle with seaweed to hold them in place until they hatch. Mother sharks wedge corkscrew-shaped eggs into rocky crevices after laying.

Sharks reach maturity much later than other fish, with species such as bull sharks and tiger sharks not reaching maturity until 10 to 15 years of age. For the Greenland shark, the age of maturity is 150 years!

Sharks are cartilaginous fish, which means that they don't have bones.

Instead, their skeletons are made up of **CARTILAGE** and connective tissue, which makes them lighter and more flexible than most other fish, and able to swim faster.

GREAT WHITE SHARK

SAND TIGER SHARK

Sharks shed an enormous number of teeth – some species can go through 30,000 teeth over their lives.

Shark's scales, called **DERMAL DENTICLES**, are more like teeth than the scales of other fish. These denticles help sharks hunt by decreasing drag and turbulence from the water.

The great white shark can swim at speeds of up to 25 kilometres per hour.

Sharks have strong senses that help them find **PREY**. In some species, nearly a quarter of a shark's brain is dedicated to smell. Sharks are also very sensitive to sound and can see in almost every direction. They often use their teeth to test objects that interest them — not good for any unintended prey.

BLACKTIP REEF SHARK

Sharks possess rows of pores called lateral lines that run from snout to tail. These lateral lines detect changes in water pressure that allow sharks to anticipate obstacles and prey.

Sharks have an extra sense that helps them track prey at close range. Mucus-filled pores on their snouts — called the Ampullae of Lorenzini — allow them to feel the tiny electrical fields produced by living creatures at close range.

This is called **ELECTRORECEPTION**.

AMPULLAE OF LORENZINI

Ampullae of Lorenzini might also serve as an internal compass, allowing sharks to navigate for thousands of kilometres using the Earth's **MAGNETIC FIELD**.

ANCIENT ROCK ENGRAVING OF A SHARK IN NORTH BONDI, SYDNEY

For Aboriginal and Torres Strait Islander coastal groups, sharks represent totems, ancestors and sometimes gods. The many shark species can embody qualities such as bravery and fearlessness.

As apex predators, sharks are seen as symbols of law and order and play a pivotal role in ceremonial events. Dreaming stories tell how different types of sharks engage in the ritual creation of the world — the gulfs, rivers and even certain trees.

Sharks are top predators and play a vital role in the ecosystem through direct and indirect predation. The presence of sharks changes the behaviour and distribution of other species. Scientists call this the 'landscape of fear'. Unfortunately, some shark populations have declined significantly in the past 50 years and many species are now **ENDANGERED**.

It is estimated that humans are responsible for approximately 100 million shark deaths each year. Sharks are hunted for their liver oil, skin, meat and fins.

The single biggest threat to sharks is overfishing. While there are fisheries that target sharks, the majority of sharks are caught as **BYCATCH**. Many animals, including turtles, dolphins and whales, are also caught and killed as bycatch.

Other risks to sharks include ocean plastic, pollution from toxins and heavy metals, climate change and habitat loss.

BULL SHARK

Despite international promises to protect the world's oceans, only about 3 percent are currently protected from fishing and mining. Australia has one of the largest marine protection networks in the world, with 15 percent of its oceans fully protected.

You can help to protect shark populations and ocean BIODIVERSITY by avoiding health and beauty products that contain shark liver oil (squalene), buying sustainably sourced seafood, avoiding shark meat (often called flake) and avoiding restaurants selling shark fin soup.

Other important efforts include reducing ocean plastic, setting catch limits and working towards climate action.

The largest shark to ever live was the megalodon, which ruled the ocean between 3.6 and 20 million years ago. Its teeth could be up to 18 centimetres long. The megalodon is estimated to have been up to 20 metres long, and about 14 metres on average — more than 3 times the length of the modern great white shark. The megalodon probably hunted whales.

WHALE SHARK

DID YOU KNOW ...

The name 'shark' is thought to come from the Dutch word for 'villain' or 'scoundrel'.

Most sharks live between 20 and 30 years, but the Greenland shark can live for nearly 300 years.

Some species of shark must swim continuously in order to breathe. These sharks can swim while unconscious, a process known as sleep swimming.

Sharks belong to the subclass Elasmobranchii, referring to their broad, flattened gills. This group also includes rays.

Sharks were once known to mariners as 'sea dogs'. This is why we have species named dogfish, smoothhounds and porbeagles.

Sharks come in various colours, mostly for **CAMOUFLAGE**. Great whites and mako sharks are shades of grey, which disguises them in open water. The nurse shark uses its brown colour to blend in on the seafloor. The wobbegong can disguise itself as rocks or even coral.

GLOSSARY

Aggregate: among sharks, aggregation refers to gatherings of sharks not motivated by social interaction (for example, to feed).

Biodiversity: the variety of plants, animals and other species in an ecosystem.

Bycatch: animals caught unintentionally in nets along with the targeted fish.

Cartilage: a firm, flexible connective tissue. In many animals it helps to protect joints, but sharks and other cartilaginous fish have a skeleton composed entirely of cartilage.

Camouflage: using shape, colour and texture to blend into the landscape.

Dermal Denticles: tooth-like structures made up of a pulp cavity surrounded by dentine and enamel-like substances.

Ecosystem: a community of living things interacting with and dependent upon one another and their environment.

Electroreception: a sense used to detect electric fields.

Endangered: a species at risk of extinction.

Fertilisation: the fusion of hereditary material from two different cells.

Magnetic field: an invisible field of force surrounding the planet or magnetic objects. Compasses work by aligning with the Earth's magnetic field.

Prey: an animal hunted for food by other animals.

Species: a population of living things capable of reproducing.